Imitating *Nature*

From Lizard Saliva
to Diabetes Drugs

Other books in this series include:

Imitating *Nature*

From Lizard Saliva *to Diabetes* Drugs

Toney Allman

KIDHAVEN PRESS

An imprint of Thomson Gale, a part of The Thomson Corporation

THOMSON

™

GALE

Detroit • New York • San Francisco • San Diego • New Haven, Conn. • Waterville, Maine • London • Munich

LIBRARY OF CONGRESS CATALOGING-IN-PUBLICATION DATA

Allman, Toney.
    From lizard saliva to diabetes drugs / by Toney Allman.
       p. cm. — (Imitating nature)
    Includes bibliographical references and index.
    ISBN 0-7377-3487-6 (hard cover : alk. paper)
    1. Diabetes—Treatment—Juvenile literature. 2. Gila monster—Juvenile literature. 3. Saliva—Juvenile literature. I. Title. II. Series.
    RC660.5.A34 2006
    616.4'62061—dc22

    2005023386

Printed in the United States of America

Contents

CHAPTER 1

The Gila Monster

A big, ugly, poisonous lizard lives in parts of the American Southwest. It is called the Gila monster. Gila monsters have the remarkable ability to eat huge meals and then go for months before eating again. They can do this because of an unusual substance in their **saliva**, or spit.

John Eng, a scientist and medical doctor, was fascinated by Gila monster saliva. He was trying to discover **hormones** in animals that could be used in new medicines for people. Hormones are special chemicals that keep certain body functions working properly in animals and people. Eng thought there must be a hormone in Gila monster saliva that let them eat so strangely and still stay healthy. He believed such a hormone might be useful as a medicine for people.

Dangerous Lizards

Gila monsters are desert creatures with bumpy, black and orange skin. They live in parts of Nevada, New Mexico,

The rough-skinned Gila monster lives in the deserts of the southwestern United States.

A Gila monster devours a mouse.

From Lizard Saliva to Diabetes Drugs

Utah, California, and Arizona. They can grow to be 2 feet (0.61m) long and weigh up to 12 pounds (5.4kg).

Gila monsters are one of only two kinds of poisonous lizards in the world. In their saliva is a strong poison called **venom.** When a Gila monster bites, it hangs on tightly with its powerful jaws and teeth. The venom in its saliva flows into the victim's wound. With its venom, a Gila monster can easily kill the animals it hunts for food.

Super-Size Meals

Poison is not the only chemical in Gila monster venom. Also in the lizard's saliva is the hormone that makes its strange eating habits possible.

Sometimes Gila monsters eat a lot. Other times they go for long periods without eating anything at all. Three or four times a year, a Gila monster hunts for prey and stuffs itself with eggs, birds, rabbits, and other small animals. After the giant

Eggs provide a tasty meal for a hungry Gila monster.

A Gila monster's jaws have superb gripping power. Venom glands inside its lower jaw are channeled to the sharp, grooved teeth, making its bite danerous and deadly.

From Lizard Saliva to Diabetes Drugs

meal, the lizard returns to its underground burrow and does not eat again for months. Yet the Gila monster stays perfectly healthy. No matter how much it eats or when, the Gila monster's body knows when to start **digesting** food and when to stop. What makes this possible is a hormone in the Gila monster's saliva. It signals an organ called the **pancreas** that digestion should begin or end.

Saliva Hormone Power

The pancreas makes **insulin**, a substance that helps turn food into body fuel. The hormone in Gila monster saliva signals the pancreas that the Gila monster has eaten a big meal. Then the pancreas makes insulin. The food is turned into fuel with the help of lots of insulin. When all the food is digested, the hormone tells the pancreas to stop making insulin. No more is produced until the lizard eats its next meal.

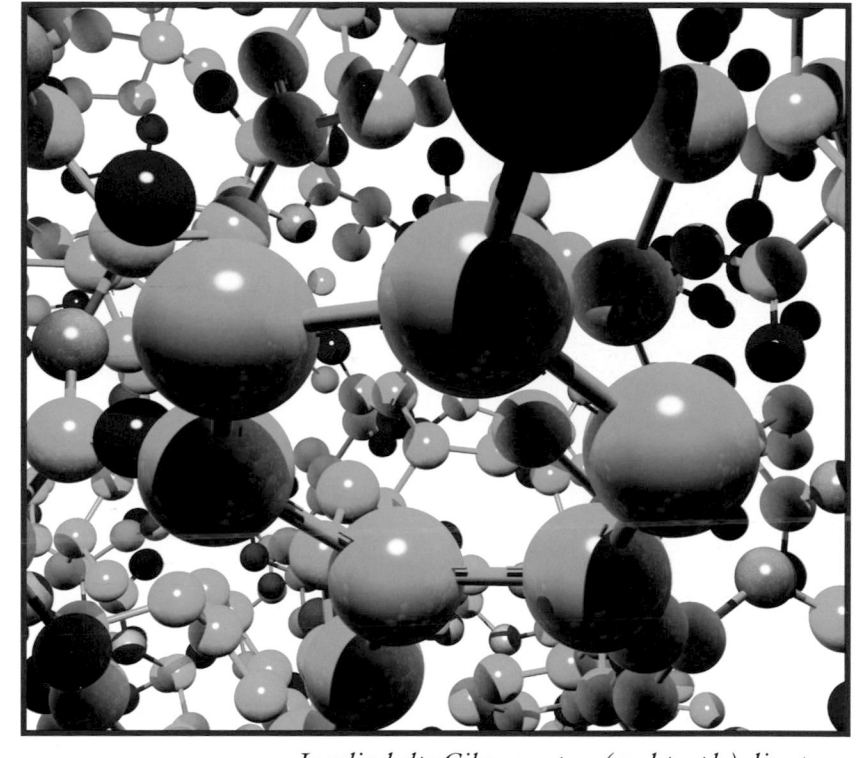

Insulin helps Gila monsters (and people) digest food. Illustrated here is a model of an insulin molecule, the chemical building block of the complex hormone.

Greedy Monsters

A Gila monster can eat a third of its weight in one meal. If a person could do that, he or she would be eating 450 double cheeseburgers at one time!

Because of the hormone in their saliva, Gila monsters never have too much or too little insulin in their bodies. Just the right amount of insulin is always available to turn food into fuel, and it is never made when it is not needed. Thanks to their spit, super-size meals are no problem for Gila monsters.

Spit for People

When Eng learned how Gila monster saliva signals the pancreas, he was fascinated. People also have pancreases that produce insulin, but sometimes they do not work correctly. Eng decided to study Gila monster saliva, find the special hormone in it, and look for a way to imitate that hormone. If he were successful, he might have a medicine that would tell people's pancreases when to function, just as lizard spit does.

From Lizard Saliva to Diabetes Drugs

CHAPTER 2

Amazing Saliva

Eng had never seen a Gila monster. He worked at the Bronx Veterans Affairs Medical Center in New York. A laboratory in Utah sent him some Gila monster saliva to study. Using what he learned from his research he hoped to make a new medicine for people who have **diabetes**.

Diabetes and Insulin

Diabetes is a disease of the pancreas. People's pancreases make insulin to help change food into body fuel, just as Gila monster pancreases do. People with diabetes, however, have pancreases that do not do their jobs correctly. The most common kind of diabetes is called type 2 diabetes. People who have type 2 diabetes do not make enough insulin at the right times. They can get very sick because their bodies need insulin every time they eat a meal.

When food is digested, it is turned into a kind of sugar called **glucose**. This sugar is carried in the blood

A Bad Disease

Diabetes is the sixth leading cause of death in the United States. If not controlled, it can lead to heart disease, kidney disease, eye damage, high blood pressure, strokes, and problems with blood circulation. In extreme cases, poor blood circulation can require amputation of the legs or feet. Even when people take good care of themselves, diabetes often gets worse over time.

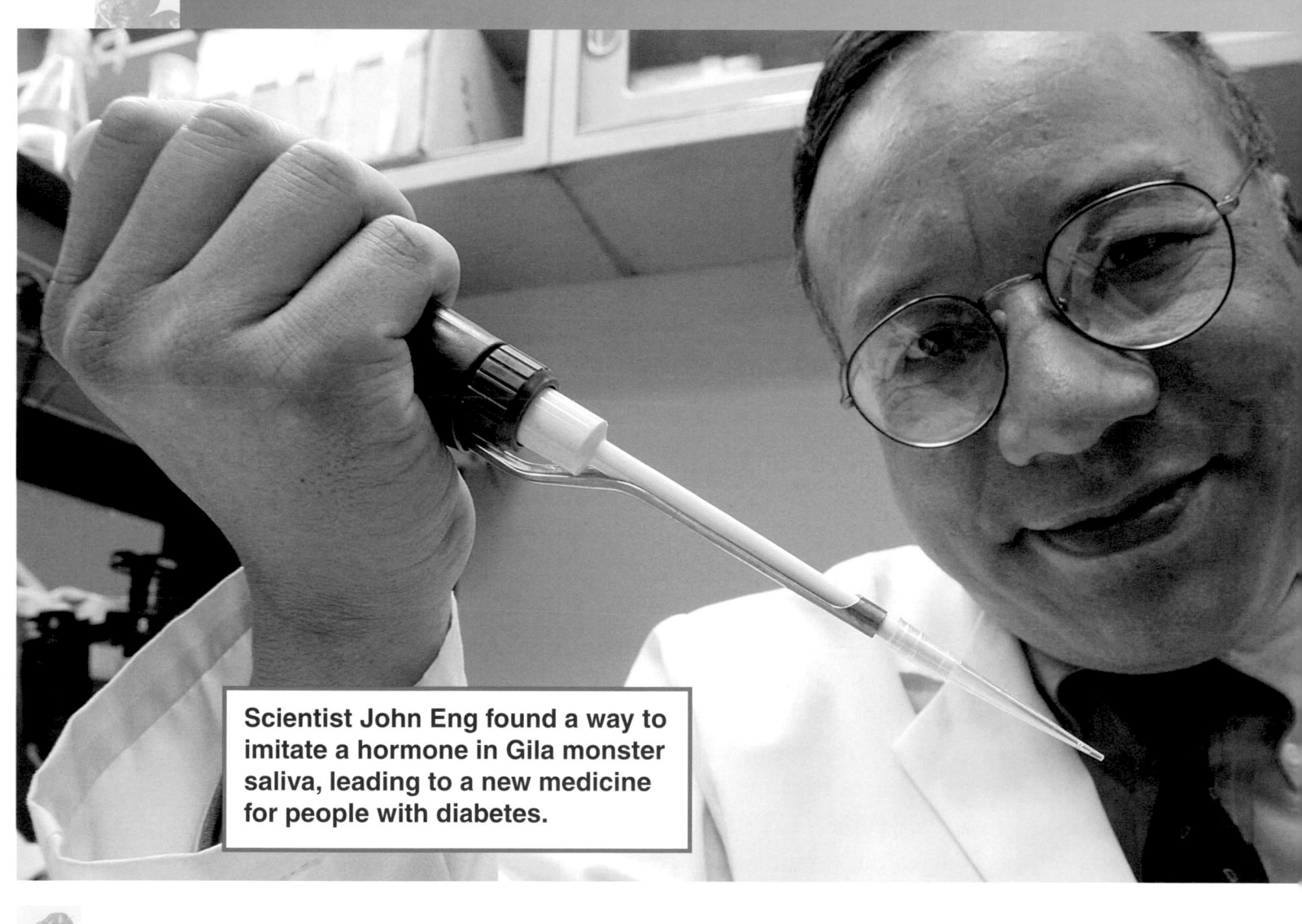

Scientist John Eng found a way to imitate a hormone in Gila monster saliva, leading to a new medicine for people with diabetes.

From Lizard Saliva to Diabetes Drugs

and brings energy to all the parts of the body. Insulin directs the glucose to all the parts of the body that need fuel. The more sugar there is in the blood, the more insulin is needed to use it, and the more insulin is sent out by the pancreas.

Looking for Signals

This insulin and glucose system does not work well for people with type 2 diabetes. The glucose in their blood gets too high and the pancreas cannot produce enough insulin. People with diabetes get very sick when their blood glucose is not controlled with insulin. They can take medicines that signal their pancreases to produce more insulin. The problem is, these pills tell the pancreas to make insulin all the time—even when no food is eaten and glucose in the blood is low. This can cause diabetics

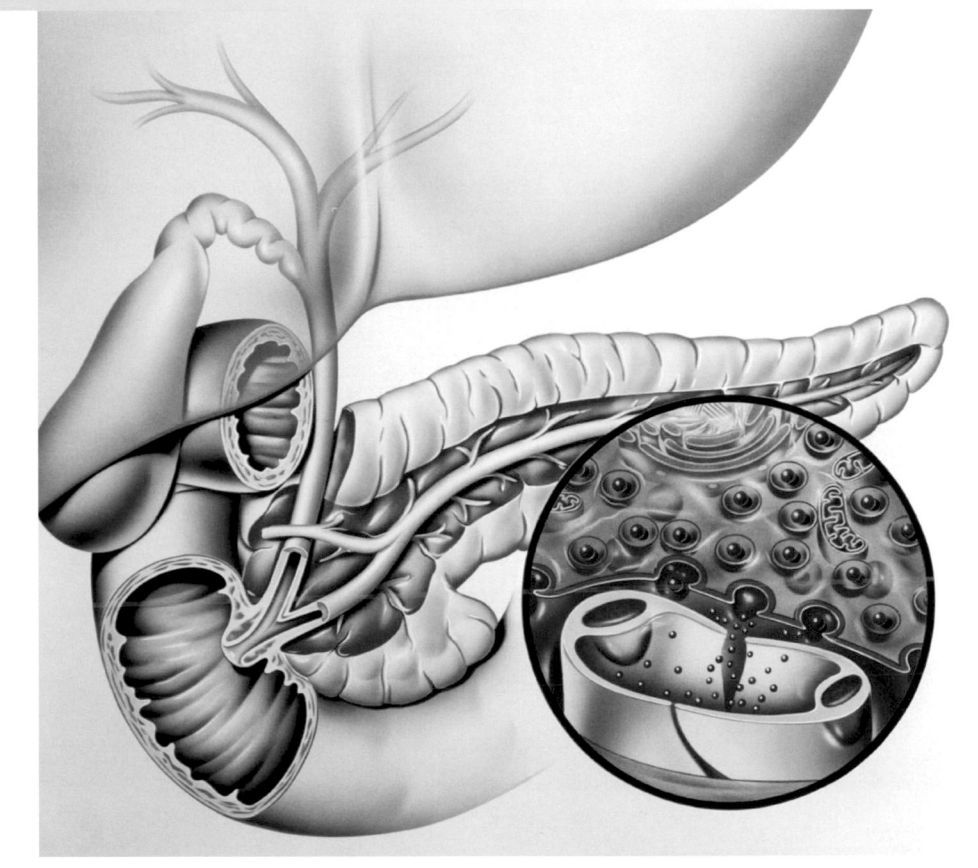

The long, leaf-shaped human pancreas makes insulin. Inside the pancreas, insulin seeps into the bloodstream through a capillary (inset).

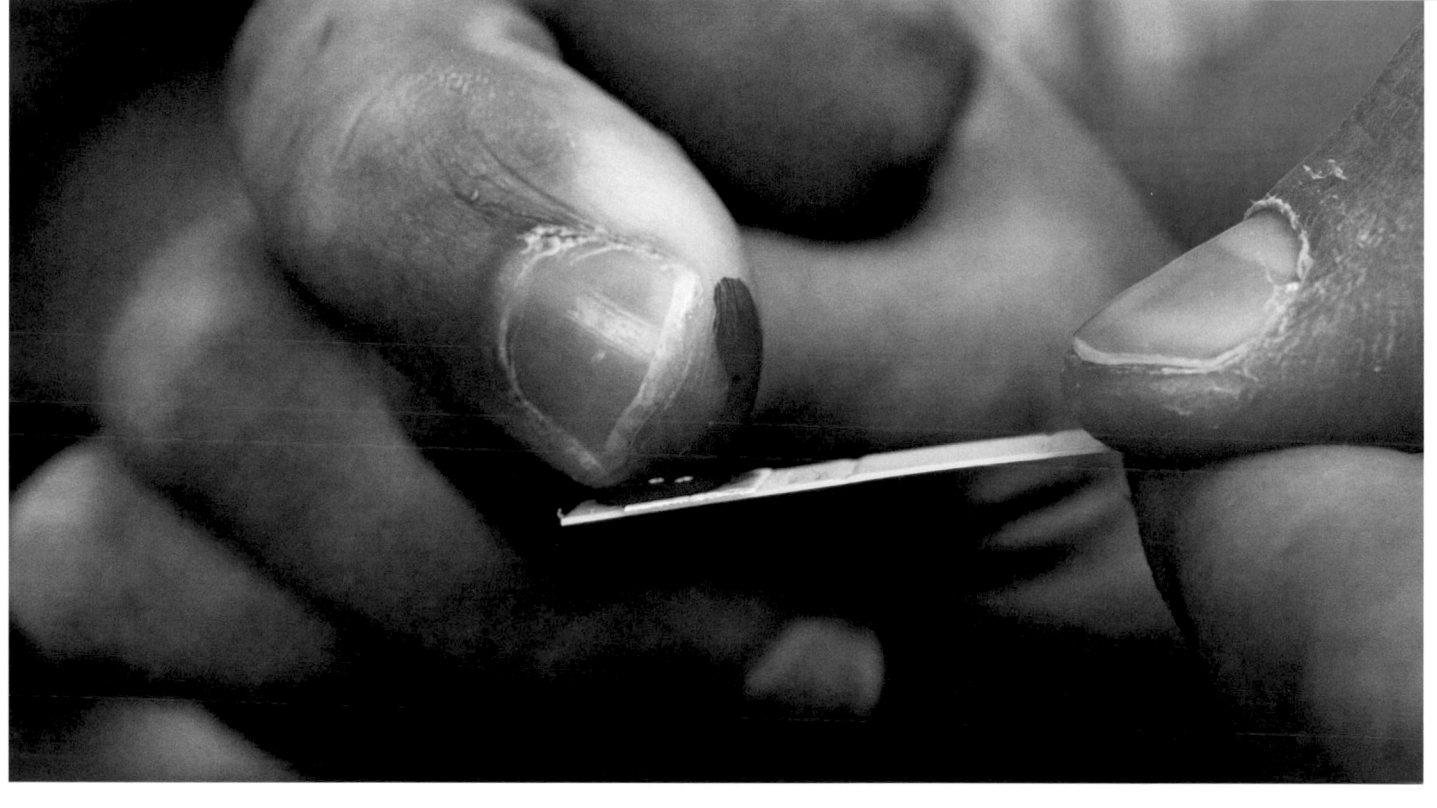

A person with diabetes pricks his finger so he can test his blood for the glucose level.

to get very sick, because the glucose in their blood is too low.

Diabetics needed a medicine that helped their glucose stay at the right level. They needed a medicine that signals the pancreas to make insulin only when it is needed. This is what Eng hoped the Gila mon-

From Lizard Saliva to Diabetes Drugs

ster saliva could do. First, however, he had to find that special hormone in the Gila monster saliva.

Exendin-4

Eng used microscopes and other specialized equipment in his laboratory to search for the hormone in Gila monster saliva. In 1992, after many experiments, he finally discovered that hormone. He named it exendin-4.

Then Eng set out to imitate exendin-4 in the laboratory. Under a microscope, he figured out the hormone's structure and copied it with chemicals from his lab. Finally he had a drug that imitated the hormone in Gila monster saliva.

Now Eng needed to know if the drug would work in people. He thought the imitation exendin-4 would signal people's pancreases to make insulin only at the right times, but he did not know for sure. In 1996 Eng joined with a drug company in California named Amylin Pharmaceuticals to test his new drug.

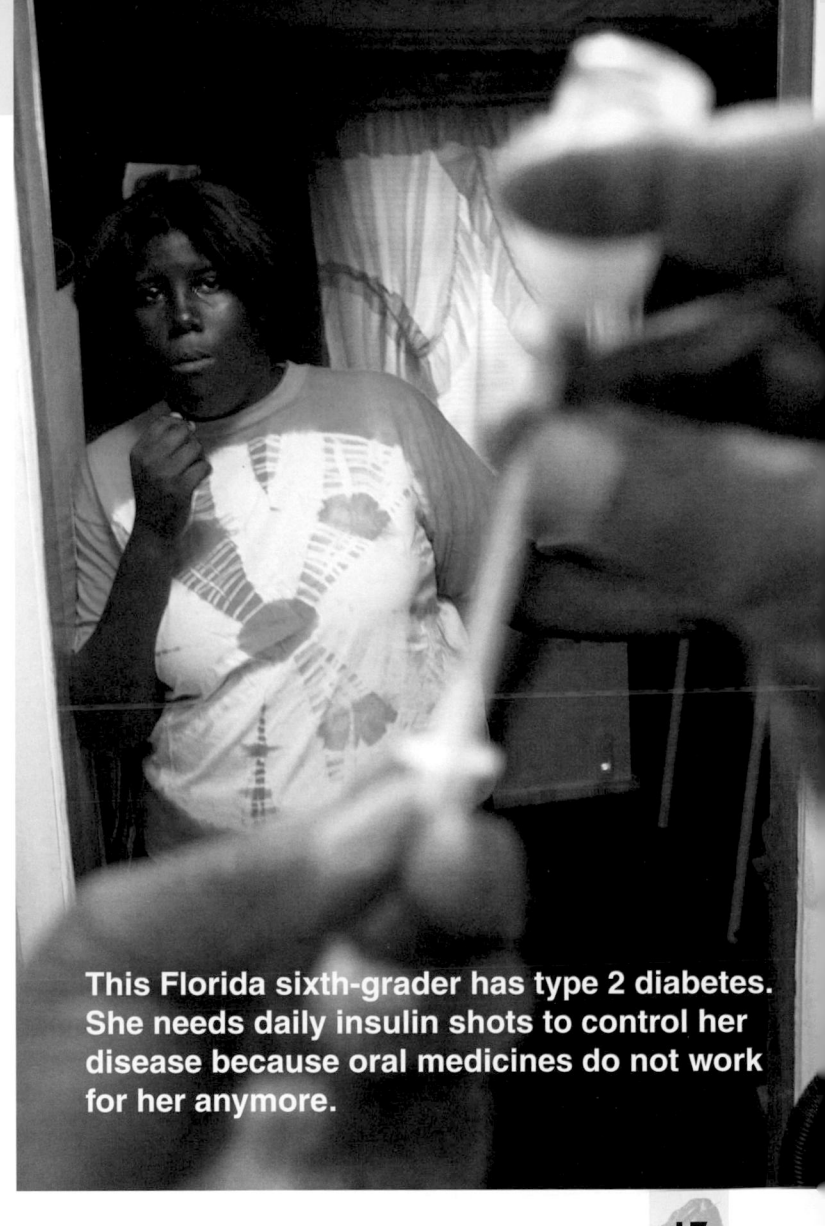

This Florida sixth-grader has type 2 diabetes. She needs daily insulin shots to control her disease because oral medicines do not work for her anymore.

Testing the New Drug

Amylin joined with another drug company, Eli Lilly, to test the new diabetes medicine. They named the new drug Byetta. For eight years Byetta was tested on animals and more than a thousand human volunteers. The experiments showed that the drug was safe for people.

Byetta seemed to signal pancreases to make insulin only when it was needed.

Amylin asked the U.S. Food and Drug Administration (FDA) to approve the new drug. In April 2005, the FDA agreed that Byetta is safe for people to use and helps diabetics control their glucose. Eng's lizard drug was a success, and doctors could try it for their patients with diabetes.

From Lizard Saliva to Diabetes Drugs

CHAPTER 3

A Drug for Diabetes

John Eng wrote the first prescription for Byetta on June 1, 2005. Since that time, thousands of people with diabetes have started using the medicine that mimics Gila monster saliva.

Taking Byetta

People with type 2 diabetes take several types of medicine to help the pancreas make insulin and to control blood glucose levels. Doctors try different combinations in hopes of getting the best results. So far, Byetta seems to do what it was designed to do. It signals the pancreas to make insulin only when sugar in the blood is high.

People give themselves two shots of Byetta a day. The shots cause no pain because the needles are very tiny, and the dose of Byetta is small. Most users say they have had good results. They find that their blood sugar is normal, and many feel better than they have in years.

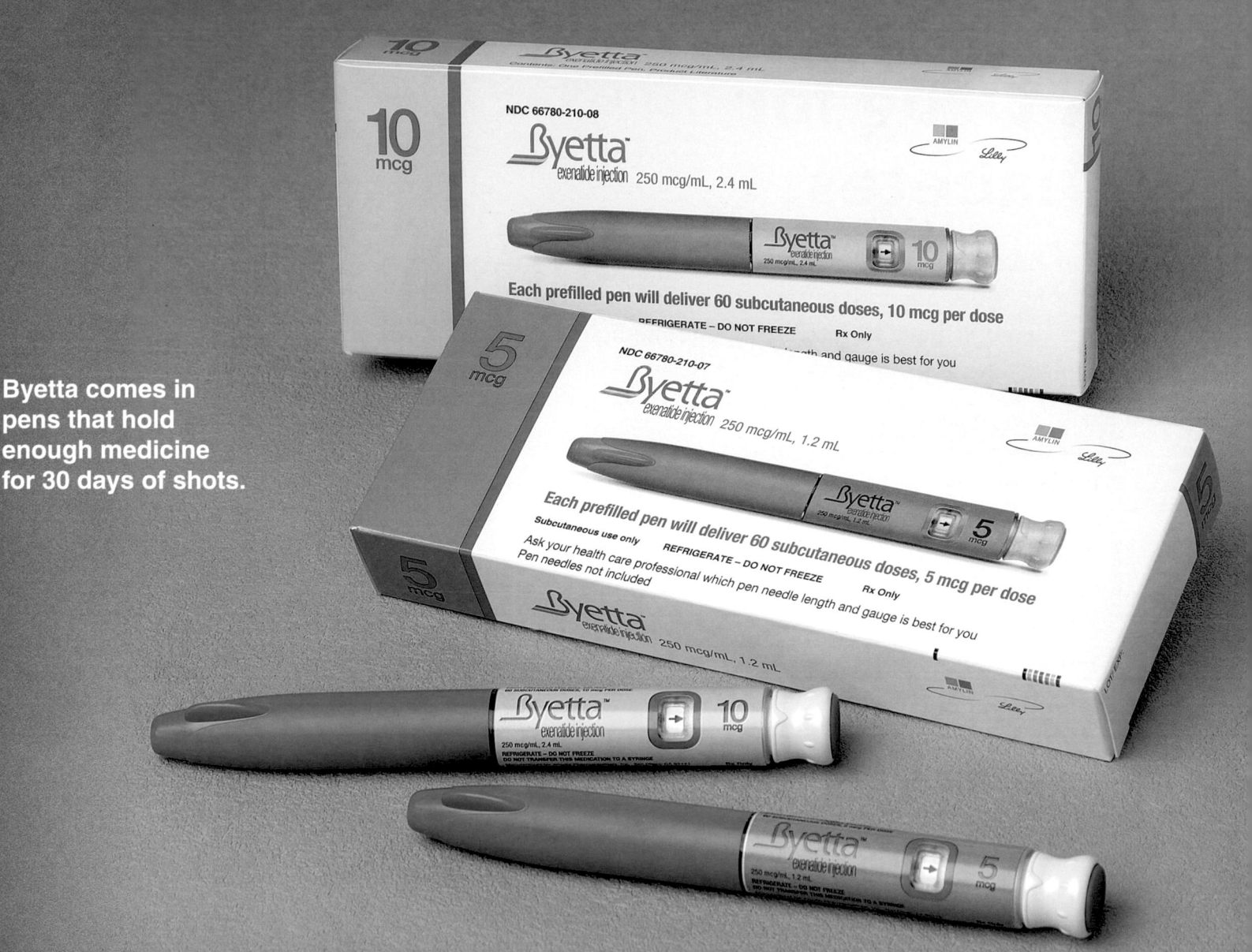

Byetta comes in pens that hold enough medicine for 30 days of shots.

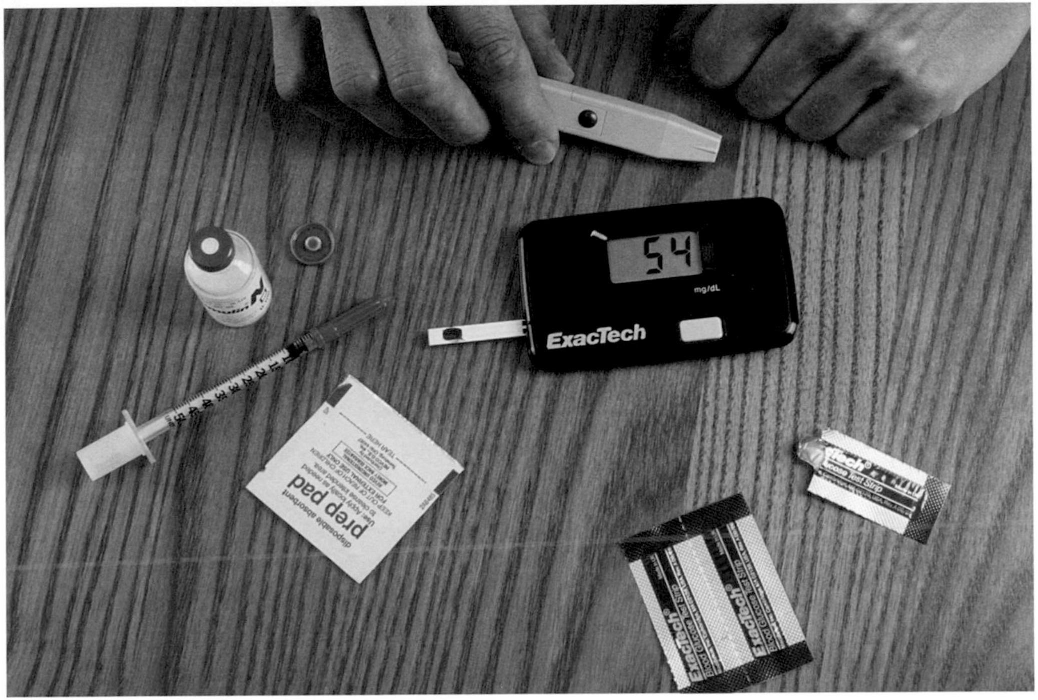

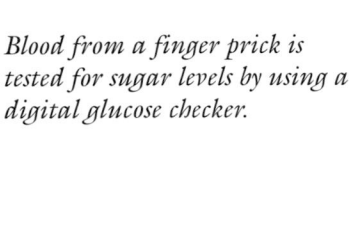

Blood from a finger prick is tested for sugar levels by using a digital glucose checker.

Seeing Results

High blood glucose levels can drop to normal within 24 hours of starting Byetta. One woman, Armenia Hawkins, of Texas, saw her high blood sugar levels become normal after just one day with the new drug. Day after day, her glucose levels stayed normal and

healthy. She was able to lower the dose of her other diabetes medicine and also had more energy than she had for a long time.

Byetta does the job diabetics hoped it would, but for many people it can be hard to get used to the Gila monster drug. About half the people taking Byetta feel sick to their stomachs and often vomit during the first weeks. Most such problems go away after a month or two, so most of the people taking Byetta stick with it despite the early problems.

Getting Healthier

Another benefit of taking Byetta is that it helps people lose weight. It makes the stomach empty more slowly than usual, so people want to eat less. This is impor-

Stomach upset is one side effect of Byetta, but the ill feeling usually goes away after a month or two.

tant for people with diabetes. The bigger a person is, the harder the pancreas has to work. Serious illnesses such as heart disease or high blood pressure can result when the pancreas works too hard.

Unfortunately, most diabetes drugs cause people to gain weight, even when they diet. Byetta does the opposite. Betty McGreevey, of Alabama began taking Byetta in July 2005. After about six months, she had lost 30 pounds (13.6kg). This gave her more energy and lowered her blood pressure so much that she was able to take less blood pressure medicine. She is full of hope that her weight loss and her improved health will continue.

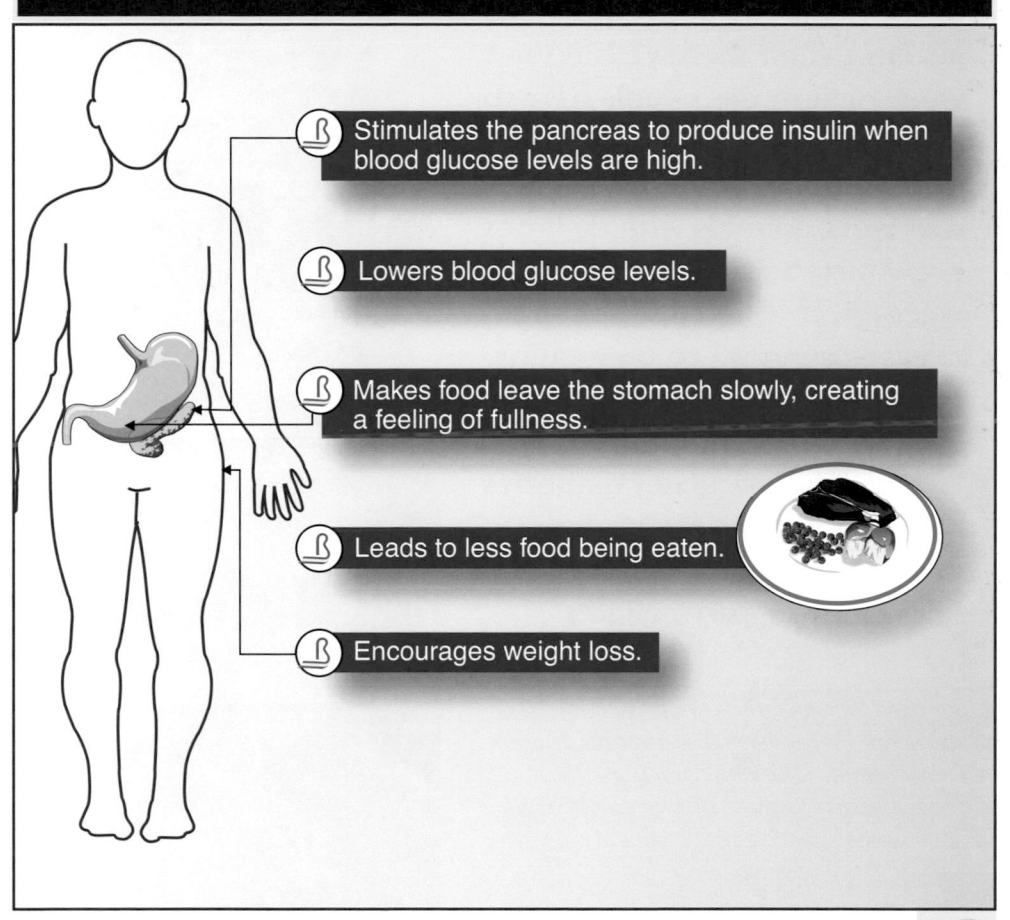

What Byetta Does in the Body

- Stimulates the pancreas to produce insulin when blood glucose levels are high.
- Lowers blood glucose levels.
- Makes food leave the stomach slowly, creating a feeling of fullness.
- Leads to less food being eaten.
- Encourages weight loss.

Hope for Pancreases

In the pancreas, beta cells make insulin. When these cells do not work right or die, people have to take insulin pills or shots to stay healthy. In some of Amylin's animal tests, animals with diabetes grew new beta cells when they were given Byetta. Their pancreases seemed to be healing. No one knows if people's pancreases can grow beta cells with Byetta. Thousands of diabetics will have to take Byetta for several years before doctors can know its long-term effects.

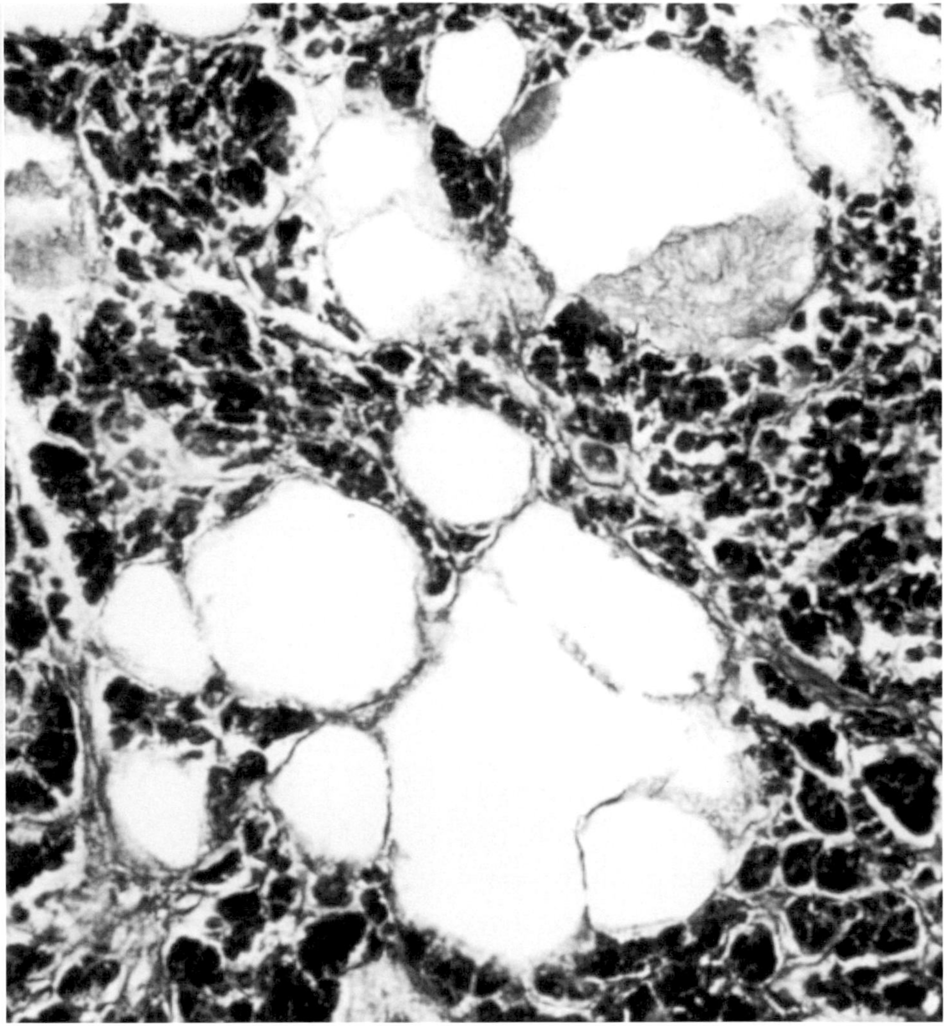

Magnified 50 times, this image from a diabetic's pancreas shows how hurt the organ's cells can become. The white places are the damaged areas where no insulin can be made.

No one knows yet if people taking Byetta will keep losing weight. Diabetics and their doctors will have to wait and see. For now, though, many diabetics call Byetta a miracle because of the way it helps to control their diabetes. McGreevey says that she knows she would be in trouble if she kissed a poisonous Gila monster but she loves the lizard just the same!

Hope from Lizard Spit

Eighteen million people in the United States have diabetes, and they struggle every day with the problems it causes. Thanks to Gila monster spit, people with type 2 diabetes may soon lead happier, healthier, and more comfortable lives.

Diabetics usually have to test their glucose levels several times per day. People taking Byetta often find that the sugar in their blood is normal.

Glossary

diabetes: A disease of the pancreas that causes glucose, or sugar, to build up in the blood. There are two kinds of diabetes—type 1 and type 2. In type 1 diabetes, no insulin is produced by the pancreas. In type 2, not enough insulin is produced at the right times.

digesting: Breaking down and changing food into a form that can be used by the body as fuel.

glucose: A sugar that is the main source of energy for the body.

hormones: Chemical substances, made by specialized body cells, that are sent through the bloodstream to another part of the body to aid and control its cell functions.

insulin: A hormone that enables the body to use sugar.

pancreas: An organ in the body that helps the body digest food and produces insulin. The pancreas is about the size of a fist and is located behind the stomach.

saliva: The watery fluid in the mouth; spit.

venom: A poisonous fluid that can be injected from one animal into another.

For Further Exploration

Books

Margery Facklam, *Lizards Weird and Wonderful*. New York: Little, Brown, 2003. This book covers the amazing world of thirteen different kinds of lizards. It shows a lizard that can kill a horse, a lizard that bleeds on purpose, and a Gila monster swallowing a meal.

Jake Miller, *The Gila Monster*. New York: PowerKids, 2003. This book discusses the Gila monster's life in its natural environment. The deadly lizard and its behavior are described, both in words and with color photographs.

Carol Antoinette Peacock, Adair Gregory, and Kyle Carney Gregory, *Sugar Was My Best Food: Diabetes and Me*. Morton Grove, IL: Albert Whitman, 1998. This is the true story of an eleven-year-old boy with diabetes. He describes the time he was diagnosed, at age nine, and how he learned to live with his disease.

Gail B. Stewart, *Diabetes*. San Diego: KidHaven, 2003. This book covers the causes and treatments of diabetes, as well as how people cope with the disease and the hope for treatments of the future.

Web Sites

Children with Diabetes (www.childrenwithdiabetes. com/index_cwd.htm). This is an online community for children and families coping with diabetes. The site has stories, chat rooms, information, and even jokes.

Dr. Mark Seward's Gila Monster Web Site (www. drseward.com/index.html). This large site is devoted to Gila monsters, their lives, their needs, and their value. Of special interest is the description of myths and superstitions about Gila monsters. There are many interesting photos of Gila monsters and the way they live.

Gila Monster (www.enchantedlearning.com/cgi-bin/paint/cvvzlycvB8mc/subjects/reptiles/lizard/Gilamonster.shtml). This site has facts about Gila monsters, and visitors can color an online picture of the lizard.

Type 2 Diabetes: What Is It? (http://kidshealth. org/kid/health_ problems/gland/type2. html). This site, written for kids, describes type 2 diabetes and explains the causes, symptoms, and treatments. Visitors can click on the links to learn much more about diabetes, glucose, insulin, and the pancreas.

From Lizard Saliva to Diabetes Drugs

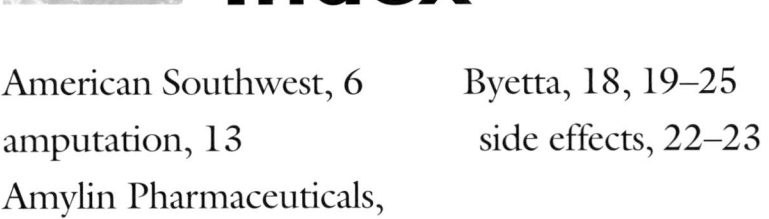

Index

Picture Credits

Cover: (from left to right) Stone/Getty Images; © Jim
Merli/Visuals Unlimited; AP Wide World Photos;
Courtesy ELI LILLY AND COMPANY
AP Wide World Photos, 14
Alfred Pasieka / Photo Researchers, Inc., 11
Astrid & Hanns-Frieder Michler/Photo Researchers, Inc., 24
Corel Corporation, 8
Courtesy ELI LILLY AND COMPANY, 20
© Jim Merli/Visuals Unlimited, 9, 10
John Bavosi/Photo Researchers, Inc., 15
© Mark Richards/CORBIS, 17
Maury Aaseng, 23
© PHOTOTAKE Inc./Alamy,
PR NewsWire ELI LILLY AND COMPANY, 18
© Roger Ressmeyer/CORBIS, 16
Stone/Getty Images, 7, 12
© U. Kaiser/zefa/CORBIS, 22
Will & Deni McIntyre/Photo Researchers, Inc., 21

About the Author

Toney Allman holds degrees from Ohio State University and the University of Hawaii. She currently lives in Virginia, where she sometimes sees lizards but luckily has never met a Gila monster.